TENBY POST

TENBY POSTCARDS
OF YESTERYEAR

Brian Cripps

First Impression—June 1995

ISBN 1 85902 295 2

Printed by
J. D. Lewis & Sons,
Gomer Press,
Llandysul, Dyfed.

To my son Kevin
whose love of Tenby
encouraged the assembling
of this collection

INTRODUCTION

Over a period of 40 years, between 1895 and 1935, the burgeoning seaside resort of Tenby attracted the attention of many skilled photographers and postcard publishers, following the publication of the first picture postcards in 1894. Of the twenty-eight or so individual photographers and publishing companies who produced cards of the historic town, the following ten were locally based: Charles Smith Allen; Henry Mortimer Allen;

Arthur Squibbs (1876-1952) and Helen Thompson, who ran the Pembroke Dock Studio.

Arthur Squibbs; F. A. Gay; John Maclaren; J. H. Hodges; G. R. Hughes; D. E. Evans; Hassall of Tenby; and Farley of Tenby. All have left us invaluable images of the Tenby of yesteryear but the work of Charles Mortimer Allen and his son Henry Mortimer, and Arthur Squibbs was of a very high quality.

Arthur Squibbs (1876-1952) and his brother Harold of Bridgewater, Somerset, came to South Wales to further their photographic careers in about 1901 and established

The Squibbs brothers, Harold and Arthur, *c.* 1920.

a studio in George Street, New Quay, on the shores of Cardigan Bay. Some years later, Arthur established other studios at Charles Street, Milford Haven; Pembroke Dock; and Warren Street, Tenby, his principal studio. At the two latter locations he was assisted by the twin sisters Helen and Kitty Thompson. Indeed, Kitty, who took up her post about 1919, was employed at the Warren Street studio until 1952, when the business was sold.

Arthur Squibbs' early Tenby work involved taking photographs not only of family and wedding groups, football and cricket teams, but also of the annual Holiday Fellowship groups who provided him with regular work during the busy summer season. During the 1914-18 war he was based at Pembroke Dock where he was engaged in photographing military personnel and new dockyard installations. However, he devoted the greater part of his life to taking picture-postcard views of beauty spots, street and beach scenes in the Tenby area. He amassed over 2,000 black-and white negatives.

In addition to local publishers, the following companies also published postcards of Tenby between 1900 and 1960: Francis Frith, Reigate; Valentine & Co., Dundee; Raphael Tuck & Sons Ltd., London; Pelham Series, Boots Chemists; Davidson Brothers, London; E. T. W. Dennis, London; Judges Ltd., Hastings; Salmon Ltd., Sevenoaks; Cambria Series, Monmouth; Senior & Co., Bristol; Aerofilms Ltd., Hendon; Northern Airlines Ltd.; Lily-White Ltd., Halifax; Stewart & Woolf, London; E. Mack, London; Regent Publishing Co., London; Hardings, Bristol; Photochrome Ltd., London.

* * *

Postcard collecting (deltiology) has become the world's second largest hobby and collectors like myself

From left to right: Kitty Thompson (b, 1906), Arthur Squibbs, Arthur (grandson, b. 1937), Millie Squibbs and Harold Squibbs (young Arthur's parents), photographed at Saundersfoot in 1947.

inevitably identify subject areas worthy of closer study. Gathering together pictures of Tenby has been a joy, and I sincerely hope that the reader will likewise enjoy the walk down memory lane, and marvel at the skill of the postcard photographers, whilst turning the pages of this book.

The work, however, would not have been possible without the assistance of others. I am sincerely grateful to many fellow collectors and dealers for their help in building up this Tenby collection. I acknowledge my sincere thanks to David Hughes and his son Steven, of Burry Port; Kitty Thompson of Tenby, former employee at Arthur Squibbs' Warren Street Studio; and Arthur Squibbs, the Hon. Secretary of the Tenby Lifeboat and his namesake's grandson.

Brian Cripps

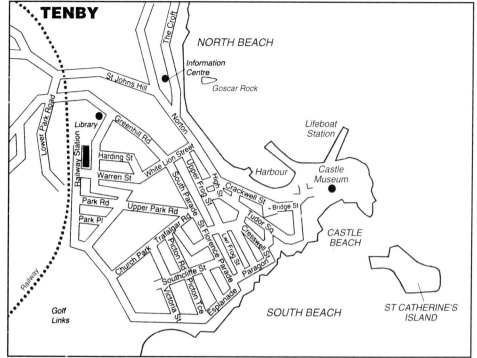

TENBY

The Croft
NORTH BEACH
Information Centre
Goscar Rock
St Johns Hill
Lower Park Road
Library
Greenhill Rd
Railway Station
Harding St
White Lion Street
Warren St
Upper Frog St
South Parade
High St
Crackwell St
Harbour
Lifeboat Station
Castle Museum
Bridge St
Park Rd
Upper Park Rd
Park Pl
Tudor Sq
Trafalgar Rd
St Florence Parade
Lwr Frog St
Cresswell St
CASTLE BEACH
Church Park
Picton Rd
Southcliffe St
Picton Tce
Paragon
Esplanade
Victoria St
Railway
Golf Links
SOUTH BEACH
ST CATHERINE'S ISLAND

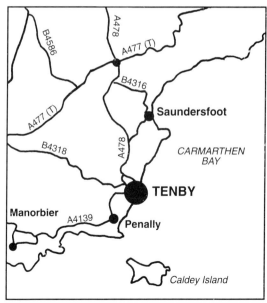

B4586
A478
A477 (T)
B4316
A477 (T)
Saundersfoot
A477 (T)
B4318
A478
CARMARTHEN BAY
Manorbier
A4139
TENBY
Penally
Caldey Island

H. Mortimer Allen's superb photograph of old houses close to Tenby harbour, *c.* 1890.

The Excelsior photographic studio, built by Charles Smith Allen in 1875, is clearly visible centre foreground. The studio is supported by angle iron, above the harbour wall. The card is dated *c.* 1895.

A postcard by Hassall of Tenby, postmarked June 1907, depicting the *William and Mary Devey* lifeboat being launched down the ramp in August 1905. The vessel was taken out of service in 1923.

North Beach and Goscar Rock with Tenby harbour in the background. The photograph is by H. Mortimer Allen, *c.* 1912.

An early coloured court card of South Beach, Tenby, and Manorbier Castle, *c.* 1898. The card is postmarked Tenby, July 1902.

An early view of Tenby in the days when you wrote your message on the picture-side of the postcard, postmarked May 1901.

The Bush Inn and the Five Arches, Tenby, *c.* 1900. The card conveyed the simple message 'Good Morning'!

Two nuns talking to a well dressed Victorian lady in Tenby High Street, *c.* 1899.

H. Mortimer Allen's viewcard is of the Imperial Hotel in the Paragon, *c.* 1912.

Tenby harbour and North Beach. This card, postmarked 1900, also clearly depicts the photographic studio built by Charles Smith Allen, father of H. Mortimer Allen (see p. 2).

The fifteenth-century Tudor merchant's house in Quay Hill, near Tudor Square, Tenby, *c.* 1904.

St. Mary's church and a traffic-free High Street in 1916.
The open brake is parked in Tudor Square.

An H. Mortimer Allen card of the Royal Gatehouse
Hotel, Tenby, *c.* 1911.

Children selling fish and lobsters outside the Griffiths' Temperance Hotel, Quay Hill, *c.* 1907. The gable end of the Tudor merchant's house stands in the background.

A 1936 viewcard of the Cliffe Hotel published by Squibbs' Studios, Tenby.

A pleasure steamer moored at Tenby harbour pier, *c.* 1913. The photograph is by H. Mortimer Allen.

A holiday postcard of the Norton and Cliffe Hotels, postmarked 1947.

This superb photograph of Lexton Terrace and Castle Beach, Tenby, by Mortimer Allen is postmarked 1913.

H. Mortimer Allen's card of Warren Street and the Congregational Church, *c.* 1910.

This Valentine series postcard of the Jubilee Walk above South Beach, Tenby, is postmarked July 1924.

Whatever was taking place on the South Beach, below St Catherine's Island, it attracted the attention of a large crowd.

The Seamen's Mission, Tenby

St Julian's Seamens' mission chapel, situated alongside the harbour, was opened in 1878. The card is dated *c.* 1912.

A rare postcard of a beach launching of the Tenby lifeboat, possibly the *Annie Collin*, in 1903.

A splendid family group taken at Castle Hill, Tenby, by H. Mortimer Allen, *c.* 1910. Note the wooden sand-spades and superb Edwardian costumes.

Campbells' paddle steamer at Tenby harbour pier taking on passengers in 1958.

Edwardian gentlemen and mechanics pose in front of a motor car, *c.* 1908. This photograph by H. Mortimer Allen was probably taken outside Ace Garages, Tenby.

The Royal Victoria pier, opened in 1899, was popular amongst holiday makers until it was demolished in 1953. This card is postmarked 1904.

Visiting trawlers from Milford (M) and Dartmouth (DH) in Tenby harbour, *c.* 1904.

A rare view of Ivy Cottages near Cresswell Street, c. 1907. In the centre background is the spire of St Mary's church.

Tenby, North Sands.

Bathing machines on the North Beach all bear adverts for Pears soap. Many well-dressed people are seen taking a constitutional stroll along the beach but few have ventured into the sea.

A superb H. Mortimer Allen postcard of the French pilot M. Salmet in his monoplane on the South Beach, Tenby, 1912. Also in the picture are Ivy Ace, her father (Ace Garages) and Reg Farley. The flight was sponsored by the *Daily Mail* newspaper.

The war memorial and palm trees at the corner of Upper Park Road, Tenby, *c.* 1935.

28

This High Street view by H. Mortimer Allen is of the Tenby Meet in 1913. Many horses but no hounds!

Tenby harbour at low tide in 1926. The prominent buildings on the left are Paxton's old bath houses, now called Laston House, built in 1805. The card, published by Pelham, is postmarked 1926.

A rare H. Mortimer Allen postcard of South Beach, Tenby. Could the Edwardian tripods and camera be some of Mortimer's own equipment, and the people relaxing in the sand dunes some of the photographer's family and friends?

Tenby harbour packed with fishing trawlers from Milford and Dartmouth. The card is by Hassall of Tenby and is postmarked 1905.

A paddle steamer leaving Victoria Pier, Tenby. This Valentine series card is postmarked 1911.

A section of the west wall in Florence Parade, Tenby. Published by John Maclaren of Tenby, the card is postmarked September 1921.

Serried ranks of beach huts on the South Beach below the imposing Esplanade hotels, *c.* 1928. The postcard was published by the stationer and tobacconist, C. R. Hughes.

The Norton Hotel (centre picture) at the junction of The Croft and Crackwell Street, *c.* 1919. The card is by John Maclaren.

This fine photograph of Victoria Pier by the Davidson Brothers is postmarked 1907.

Bathing machines on Castle Beach. St Catherine's Island stands in the background. Published by the Davidson Brothers, the card is postmarked 1907.

A Davidson Brothers' card, postmarked 1907, of the ruins of Tenby Castle.

A striking view of Castle Beach and St Catherine's Island, May 1935.

The Five Arches in Florence Parade, *c.* 1907.

A lazy summer's day just messing about in boats off the North Beach, *c.* 1936.

Holy Cross + St. Teilo Tenby. S. Wales

Convent of St. Teresa

A rare view of St Teresa's Convent and the Catholic church, opposite the Five Arches, *c.* 1913.

Looking north along The Croft, *c.* 1910. No parking problems in those days!

A crowd soon gathers to oblige the street photographer who wants a picture of Five Arches from South Parade. The card is dated *c.* 1907.

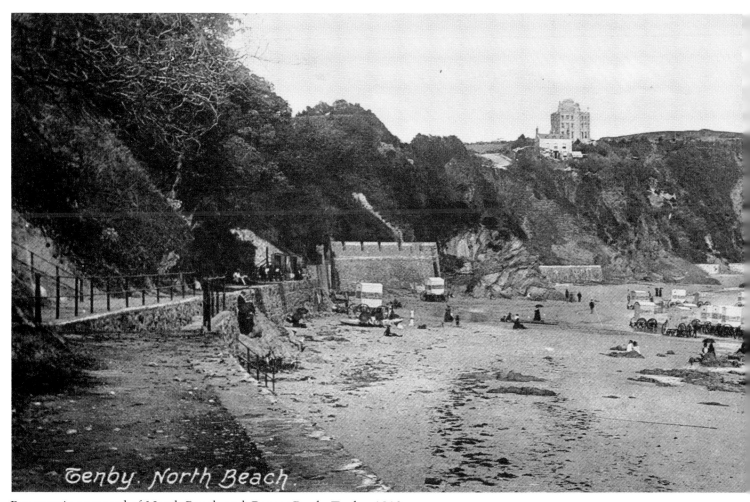

Panoramic postcard of North Beach and Goscar Rock, Tenby, 1912.

46

An aerial view of the harbour, Castle Hill and St Catherine's Island, *c.* 1932. Many holiday makers can be seen on Castle Beach.

The Esplanade and South Beach from the air. Shanly's cinema (top left) was built in 1929. The card is postmarked July 1935.

Shanly's cinema and dance hall is still under construction in this 1929 postcard. Rows of bathing huts and deckchairs can be seen on the South Beach.

An aerial view of Tenby looking north-east towards Monkstone Point. The card is postmarked July 1931.

LIFEBOAT LAUNCH. TENBY. 295

This H. Mortimer Allen card, postmarked 1915, is a photographic original and records a launching of the lifeboat *William and Mary Devey, c.* 1904.

Crowds watching a golf tournament on the Tenby Links in 1924.

Greetings from Tenby.

THE GAME OF GOLF.
Take me, Miss.

A rare Lance Thackeray golf card published by Raphael Tuck in *c.* 1908.

Greetings from Tenby.

The Game of Golf.

'The Game of Golf' card by Lance Thackeray conveying greetings from Tenby, *c.* 1908.

A comic golf card by G. E. Shepheard depicting caddies looking for a lost ball 'at Tenby'. The card was published by Raphael Tuck in *c*. 1910.

An Ilfracombe paddle steamer moored alongside the Tenby harbour pier. The card is postmarked 1923.

The military fortifications on St Catherine's Island were completed in 1870 at a cost of £26,000 and were capable of accommodating 100 troops. The card is postmarked August 1904.

This superb photograph of fishermen and children outside cottages near Tenby harbour was taken by Charles Smith Allen in 1885. This card is postmarked 1905.

Tenby town from Castle Hill (left), and the Five Arches (right), *c.* 1912.

60

This tranquil scene of the harbour and North Beach was taken in 1939.

Panoramic postcard of the harbour and town, and the coast to the south-west of Tenby, 1912.

62

Amongst the harbourside buildings in this view are Laston House (far left), the old Albion Hotel and St Julian's chapel (far right). The card is postmarked 1925.

There are no bowling greens in sight in this 1905 view of Marine Parade. The road is now called Southcliffe Street.

HIGH STREET TENBY.

A 1938 viewcard of Tudor Square and St Mary's church. The telegraph poles on the right mark the former location of Tenby's Post Office.

66

THE SLUICE, TENBY.   209011 JV

Grimsby and Milford boats moored in The Sluice, alongside the harbour, 1934.

Bathing machines galore, all advertising 'Beechams pills', on South Beach, 1907.

Lower St Julian's Street and St Julian's chapel, *c.* 1912.

Holiday makers on North Beach in September 1913. It appears that nobody has risked taking the plunge.

The launch of the Tenby lifeboat at low tide on 10 August 1908.

A J.H. Hodges card of South Beach and the Esplanade, *c.* 1910. Bathing costumes are conspicuously absent.

H. Mortimer Allen's card of the Sydney Lesters Group on stage at the De Vallence Theatre in Upper Frog Street, *c.* 1908.

De Vallence Gardens, Tenby,

The De Vallence Gardens and Theatre in Upper Frog Street was opened in 1904. This card is postmarked August 1909.

A lone postman, nurse, pedestrian and dog in Crackwell Street. The card, published by F.A. Gay, is dated *c.* 1912.

Nothing is known about this superb postcard by H. Mortimer Allen, dated *c.* 1910. Are the men in the company of the officer being held in detention? Is that a jail in the background?

Fishing boats from Milford and Dartmouth departing Tenby harbour at high tide, *c.* 1904.

Holiday makers relaxing opposite the Cobourg Hotel and Peerless Hotel in Crackwell Street, *c.* 1934. This card is by Squibbs' Studios.

An elevated view of the harbour, Castle Hill and the hotels in Castle Square. The parked cars suggest that the photograph was taken during the 1930s.

The photographer ventured out in a boat to take this fine view of bathing machines and holiday makers on North Beach, *c.* 1910. Goscar Rock is the dark form on the far left of the picture.

Another superb Squibbs' postcard of the North Beach packed with bathers, taken from the sea. In the background are the hotels along the Croft. This card is postmarked July 1933.

The ruins of St Mary's College by John Maclaren, The Library, Tenby. The card is postmarked July 1925.

Low tide at Goscar Rock on the North Beach allows lots of holiday makers to enjoy the sands. This Squibbs' card is dated *c.* 1932.

A superb view of Tudor Square published by Pelham and postmarked 1927. Apparently it was safe to walk in the middle of the road in those days!

A view of North Beach from the Peerless Hotel in Crackwell Street by Squibbs' Studio, *c.* 1934.

The Five Arches and Florence Parade. The card was published by Salmon during the 1930s.

A busy High Street scene where everyone seems to be looking at the photographer. Note the two soldiers standing on the pavement on the left-hand side of the road. This Dennis and Sons card is postmarked 1917.

A super picture of North Beach by H. Mortimer Allen and postmarked 1914. Note the Punch and Judy show and the fine Georgian costumes.

A Carmarthen-bound train picks up passengers at Tenby station, *c.* 1912. The station, built in 1866, witnessed the arrival and departure of most of the holiday makers visiting the town prior to the days of cars and caravans.

This delightful photo was taken by D. E. Evans in South Parade in September 1906. Note the officer's white helmet and the surprisingly modern looking bicycle.

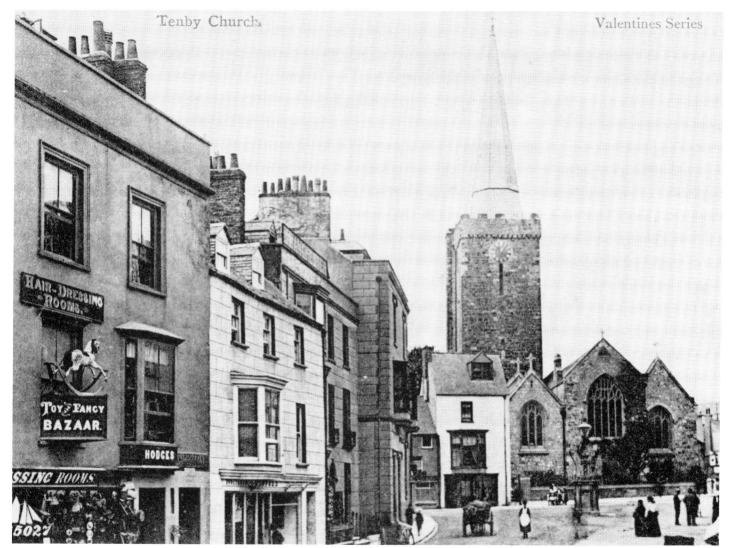

St Mary's church and Tudor Square. This card, which gives some prominence to the Hair-Dressing Rooms above Hodges fancy and toy bazaar is postmarked August 1906.

Five Arches, Tenby

The Bush Inn (left) and grocers shop (right) in St George's Street, 1917. In the background is a section of the old town wall and the Five Arches.

Two sailors and a trap can be seen in this 1909 view of South Parade by Stewart and Woolf of London.

Farley of Tenby published this card of the interior of St Mary's church in March 1921.

A packed Esplanade on a Sunday in August 1917. Several soldiers are amongst the crowd attired in their Sunday-best clothes.

A lone sailor surveys the town from his vantage point on Castle Hill, *c.* 1905.

THE BATHING BEACH, TENBY.

Bathers and bathing machines at high tide on the North Beach. No skimpy costumes in those days! Although postmarked 1926 the card was probably published in *c.* 1908.

Goscar Rock, North Beach, by H. Mortimer Allen, *c.* 1912.

Fishing boats from Dartmouth in Tenby harbour. The photograph was taken by Charles Smith Allen in 1895, but the card is postmarked 1904.

What! Come Home?
Not likely, when I'm at
TENBY.

A novelty card by E. Mack, London, and postmarked 1914.

A 1936 novelty card by Regent of London illustrating an alternative means of travelling to Tenby!

SOMETHING TELLS ME YOU'LL BE DROPPING IN TO SEE ME SOON !

AT TENBY

Tudor Square in the late 1950s.

A wonderful photograph of South Beach and hotels along the Paragon. Most of the well-dressed people seem content to chat on the sands whilst others venture to paddle. The card, by Arthur Squibbs, is postmarked May 1921.

Water Wynch, Nr Tenby

An Edwardian schoolboy, with trousers rolled up, is fascinated by the life in the rock pools along the shore at Waterwynch, north-east of Tenby, in 1904.

The Somerset and South Beach private hotels are well illustrated in this view of Victoria Street published by Squibbs about 1934.

The County School, *c.* 1908. Today the buildings are occupied by the Tenby library.

Holidays at Tenby invariably put smiles on the faces of holiday groups. This super Squibbs' card is dated August 1931.

This Holiday Fellowship group is dated 1931. The lady on the extreme left of the second row from the front apparently wished to remain anonymous!

High tide at South Beach at the foot of the limestone cliffs below the Paragon, *c.* 1916.

Florence Parade looking towards the Five Arches. The card, by H. Mortimer Allen, is dated *c.* 1910.

The hotels Continental and Peerless, and Mr Gunter's shoe shop can be seen in this view of Crackwell Street, *c.* 1910.

Tenby harbour from the Croft, *c.* 1911.

A rare view of Tenby harbour and North Beach taken from Castle Square. The card, by Arthur Squibbs, is dated *c.* 1931.

A large crowd in Tudor Square in 1919 celebrating the end of the First World War. Can you spot the Mayor and Town Crier?

Four members of Tenby Congregational Church photographed on the occasion of the Sunday School outing to Scotsboro on 16 June 1915.

Over fifty children, accompanied by parents and friends, taking part in a sand building competition on Tenby's South Beach. This H. Mortimer Allen card is dated *c.* 1910.

Tenby Golf Links and the village of Penally, 1958.

Penally church. The card by F. A. Gay is postmarked 1929.

Penally Army Camp, *c.* 1915.

Penally Camp by H. Mortimer Allen, *c.* 1914.

Between Penally and Tenby lies an embryonic Kiln Park Caravan Site and the dunes known as the Burrows. The photograph was taken in the 1930s.

Penally Village.

Penally railway station. The card is postmarked September 1905.

A fine view of the Cross Inn, Penally, with children gazing at the cameraman. This card, written from Giltar Terrace and posted in August 1915, was published by H. Mortimer Allen.

A military parade at Penally, 12 June 1914. This excellent card by H. Mortimer Allen was sent by an officer to an address near Stockport, Lancashire.

This card by J. Mortimer Allen would appear to depict First World War male internees under military guard, possibly in the Tenby area.